LETCHWOR'
GARDEN CI'
1903 - 2003

A Centenary Celebration of the World's first Garden City in Picture Postcards

3. This is an advertising postcard issued by B.P. Smith, Tailor of Station road in 1937. It was illustrated by Crombi who lived in Baldock Road.

ALL THE POSTCARDS IN THIS BOOK ARE FROM THE PERSONAL COLLECTION OF MARGARET PIERCE.

YESTERDAYS WORLD PUBLICATIONS 2002

THE LETCHWORTH DIRECTORY OF 1915

"Briefly, it was a suggestion for town building by plan and foresight as opposed to the sporadic growth of the average city. The result would be to ensure that every man, woman and child had an abundance of fresh air and sunlight and it was to be expected that good health and a higher moral tone would follow as a result."

Ebenezer Howard's vision as outlined in his book 'Garden Cities of Tomorrow' was put into practice in 1903 when 3818 acres of land in Letchworth and the surrounding area was purchased by the Garden City Association at a cost of £155,587.

This book is a collection of postcards telling the story of the development of the World's First Garden City over the last 100 years.

IN GRATITUDE

I would like to thank all the Publishers - some anonymous, and others well known for producing the following postcards of Letchworth Garden City over the last 100 years and making this book possible. I would also like to thank the photographers, without whom we would not have had the pictorial history of the world's first Garden City recorded so extensively. A special mention must go to Arthur Clutterbuck, our extremely productive local photographer who from his home in Icknield Way provided a wonderful account not only of the surroundings, but also of the social history of the Garden City. I have tried to credit all the postcards in this book and apologise to anyone not included.

I would also like to thank the following modern publishers for giving me permission to use their postcards in this book -

Hallmark Cards U.K. (Valentine)
Judges Postcards Ltd. Hastings
First Garden City Heritage Museum
Letchworth Museum, North Herts Museum Service
Letchworth Garden City Heritage Foundation for postcards issued by themselves and Letchworth Garden City Corporation.

And last, but not least, I would like to thank everyone in Letchworth and especially the Garden City Society who has been able to help me in my quest for information about our unique town.

PUBLISHED BY
YESTERDAYS WORLD PUBLICATIONS
32 Haselfoot, Letchworth Garden City, Hertfordshire, SG6 4DE
Tel: 01462 684683
Copyright MARGARET PIERCE 2002
ISBN 09542771 0 4

PRINTED BY
ADLARD PRINT & REPROGRAPHICS LIMITED
The Old School, The Green, Ruddington, Nottingham, NG11 6HH
www.adlardprint.com

4. Letchworth Garden City on a postcard by Arthur Clutterbuck postmarked in 1910

INTRODUCTION

I have been collecting postcards of Letchworth Garden City since I was a child growing up here. I came to live in the Garden City in 1957 and left when I married in 1973.

Returning to live here in 1999 I realised the town was changing rapidly and I felt all this change should be recorded. I believe the Centenary celebrations of 2003 are the perfect time to do this with my own collection of postcards.

The Garden City has been well recorded on picture postcards over the last 100 years and they clearly show how the First Garden City has developed. I hope my readers will enjoy looking at these little pictures of history as much as I have enjoyed putting then together into a book.

5. Letchworth Garden City in 1990 on a postcard by Halcyon of Bushey.

The three original villages of the Garden City estate in the early 1900's.

Coming Home from School, Letchworth Lane.

6. Letchworth Lane on a postcard by Garden City Press Series.

WILLIAN POND.

7. Willian on a postcard by Garden City Association.

Cooper's Farm, Norton (Dinner Hour).
(GARDEN CITY SERIES.)

8. Norton also on a postcard by Garden City Association.

4

Norton Church and Cottages.
(GARDEN CITY SERIES.)

9. Norton Village is of Saxon origin and has been a farming community since the 17th century. This postcard published by the Garden City Association shows St. Nicholas Church and cottages in the village from across the fields. It was postally used in 1906. It was here that the mother of the famous evangelist Gipsy Smith was buried when she died of smallpox in 1865 while camped in Norton.

10. Gipsy Rodney Smith is shown on this postcard by an unknown publisher. On the back is written - 'Gipsy Smith as a young boy at North Lane, Letchworth with his sister waving goodbye to his mother'.
He later became a famous preacher and in 1903 came back to Norton. The Methodist Mission Room in North Avenue opened in 1908 and was dedicated to the memory of his parents. His father has been buried with his wife Polly in Norton Churchyard and Gipsy Smith had a stone erected to their memory. On January 2nd 1908 he visited and probably preached at the Free Church Hall. He celebrated 60 years as a preacher by holding a large open-air service and meeting in the chalk pit at the end of Green Lane on Saturday June 20th 1936.

11. On this postcard of an idyllic scene at Willian the sender has written 'This was taken at Willian a Village about 1 mile from Garden City where my brother Albert is postman'. The publisher is Arthur Clutterbuck.

12. The Fox Inn in the village of Willian shown on a postcard posted in 1906 when the Inn was being used as a hotel and tea rooms run by the People's Refreshment House Association Ltd. of London. This postcard is by an unknown publisher.

Making New Road on Garden City Estate.

13. The Garden City Press Series postcard of early road building in Letchworth.

Garden City, 1903

14. The population of the Letchworth area in 1903 was around 400. This anonymously published postcard shows the rapid change in the town over the first 4 years and emphasises the Garden City principles of town and country side by side.

View in Norton Road Garden City. W.Ratcliffe

WILLIAN VILLAGE.

LETCHWORTH LANE GARDEN CITY W.Ratcliffe

Above

15. A view of Willian by Baldock artist Louis Weirter on a postcard issued by First Garden City Ltd. The reverse reads -

326A High Holborn
London W.C.

You can spend a pleasant and instructive holiday at Garden City, Letchworth, and see a great social experiment of national value, and hundreds of charmingly arranged and designed cottages. The present population is about 2,000. 50 minutes from King's Cross, London.

A new guide to Garden City has just been published, price 2d., post free 3d.

Full particulars from above address.

Yours truly,
Thos. Adams,
Secretary, First Garden City, Limited.

Left

16/17. Two watercolour Sketch Series postcards printed on the Garden City Estate by Garden City Press Ltd. Letchworth. The artist W.W. Ratcliffe lived on Westholm Green.

18/19. Countryside meets town - Garden City ideals shown on two rural views of the town by Frank Dean issued by the Garden City Association and postmarked 1907.

Norton Way, Letchworth.

Fence treated with Solignum.

20. An advertising postcard issued by Solignum shows houses in Norton Way. The postcard was sent from Letchworth to Belgium in 1907

Below

21. Mrs. Howard's Hall was the Garden City's first Public Building and was opened in 1906 in memory of the first wife of Ebenezer Howard. It was designed by Parker and Unwin and situated at the junction of Norton Way South and Hillshott.

Howard's Hall, Garden City, Letchworth

57687 JV

EXHIBITION OF COTTAGES, GARDEN CITY, LETCHWORTH.
MODEL COTTAGE No. 45.

22. This postcard by an unknown publisher shows an artists impression of model cottage no. 45 in the Cheap Cottages Exhibition of 1905.

It became 207 Nevells Road and was designed by A.T. Martindale.

Below

23. This view of Nevells Road was published by E. Mott of Markyate and shows newly completed numbers 212 - 217.

LETCHWORTH. GARDEN CITY. HERTS.

24. This postcard shows the opening of the Cheap Cottages Exhibition by the Duke of Devonshire on 25th July 1905. He is delivering his speech surrounded by members of the Garden City Association including Ebenezer Howard, seated on the platform far right (arrowed). This competition had a prize of £100 for the best cottage built for £150. The houses were built in Exhibition Road (below), Cross Street, The Quadant, Wilbury Road, Icknield Way, Paddock Close and Bird's Hill. The Exhibition brought the developing town much publicity and could be seen as a fore-runner of the Ideal Home Exhibition. It attracted 60,000 visitors who were able to travel to the town by Rail from King's Cross for a cheap day return ticket of 3s.5d.

25. Exhibition Road became known as Nevells Road and is shown here on a postcard published by B & D.

GARDEN CITY.   Concrete Block Cottage, Cement Products Co.   H. G. Moulden, Photo, Hitchin.

26. "The Stonehouse' 212 Nevells Road was designed by Bennett & Bidwell and constructed of textured concrete blocks to look like rough hewn stone.

27. Some Exhibition cottages including The Nook shown in Cross Street.

GARDEN CITY.   Exhibition Cottages.   H. G. Moulden, Photo, Hitchin.

Architect, Mr. G. Fraser.   Exhibit No. 58, Builders, The Concrete Machinery Co., Ltd.

GARDEN CITY, LETCHWORTH.

Exhibition of Cheap Cottages, 1905.

28. No. 4 Cross Street shown on an advertising postcard of the 1905 Exhibition. It won a special prize for the best concrete cottage, the blocks being made on site.

29. Employees of J.M. Dent & Co., Publishers, touring the Garden City on 18th May 1906 shown on a postcard by an unknown publisher.

30. Temple Gardens in Green Lane was where the Dents employees were eventually settled (named after Dent's Temple Press). It is shown here on a postcard by an unknown publisher used in 1911.

31. An early postcard of the Free Church Hall built in 1905 on the corner of Gernon Road and Norton Way South. The sign is giving directions to the Urban Cottages on Exhibition of 1907. The postcard was published by E. & E.H. Housden, Station Road.

32. This is another advertising postcard for Solignum showing the Garden City Company's offices and information kiosk for the 1907 Cottage Exhibition. This was mainly located on Lytton Avenue and this building was later converted into a house.

The Garden City Company's Offices.

(1907 Exhibition. Letchworth.)   treated with Solignum

THE SKITTLES INN, LETCHWORTH

33. The Skittles Inn opened in 1907 as a temperance establishment where only soft drinks were available. It was advertised as being for "meals, games, fellowship. A unique experiment demonstrating the value of a public-house in every way except intoxicants". This postcard was sent from a pupil at Letchworth School in 1909 and reads - 'I send a picture of the only pub in the city. All skittles and no beer. They have to go to Norton for that and the pub there is like a P.H. Trust one.'

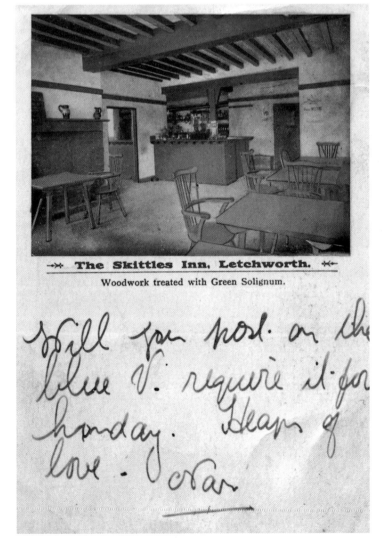

The Skittles Inn. Letchworth.

Woodwork treated with Green Solignum.

34. The interior of the Skittles Inn shown on a postcard advertising the woodwork treatment Green Solignum posted in 1908.

16

35. This cottage at 2 Cross Street (the only street in Letchworth) was an entry in the 1905. Cheap Cottages Exhibition. It took two months to build from breeze concrete on the lattice framework. Reverse details - the woodwork of the cottage in the illustration, inside and out, has been treated with Solignum. Send trial order to Major & Co. Ltd., Hull.

GARDEN CITY, LETCHWORTH.
Architect, GEORGE E. CLARE, M.S.A., 1, West Street, Finsbury Circus, London, E.C.

NORTON WAY, GARDEN CITY

36. 355-361 Norton Way South, a Parker & Unwin design of 1905 Ebenezer Howard lived in the second house from the left from 1905 till 1911. The reverse carries an advertisement for the Co-operative Permanent Building Society, 22 Red Lion Square, London W.C.

37. A view of Wilbury Road showing no.158 designed by Brodie and other houses included in the cheap Cottages Exhibition of 1905 on a postcard by Valentines.

Wilbury Road, Letchworth Garden City

38. The Cloisters opened in 1907.

39. Miss Annie Lawrence had the Cloisters built as a centre for Theosophical meditation and study. Plays, pageants and concerts were held there and on this postcard a summer school is shown in session.

40. All three postcards are photographs by local photographer Arthur clutterbuck. This one shows the beds used by the students which were pulled up during the day. This postcard was issued by Housden of Station Road, Letchworth.

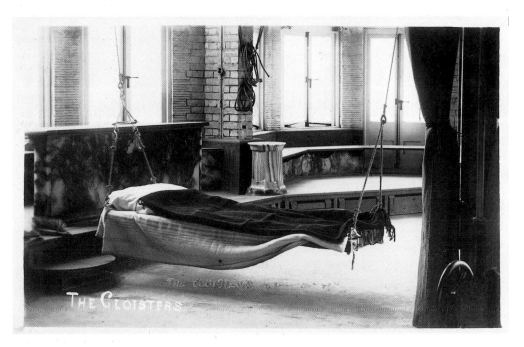

The Cloisters, Letchworth

Swimming Bath, The Cloisters, Letchworth

41. The Swimming Pool at the Cloisters was very popular with local children who were rewarded with a fountain pen for swimming across the pool. The open-air Concert Hall and the Swimming Pool are shown here on a postcard by Valentines.

The Cloisters, Letchworth Garden City

42. This is also a Valentines postcard showing the Cloisters and adjoining house.

19

S 6399   WESTHOLM GREEN, LETCHWORTH GARDEN CITY.

43/44. Shown here are postcards of Westholm and Eastholm Greens issued by Kingsway. Westholm, facing Norton Common was designed by Parker & Unwin as a self-contained cottage development for Garden City Tenants, a Housing Society which built modest rented accommodation for industrial workers. The houses were built around a central green which was originally closed off with gates. Eastholm was also a Parker & Unwin design and both sites were developed in 1905-6.

S 6392   EASTHOLM GREEN, LETCHWORTH GARDEN CITY.

45. This postcard shows some of the early houses in Sollershott West. The sender has marked her home with a cross. This is also a Kingsway postcard and all three were postally used in 1910.

S 6397   SOLLERSHOTT W, LETCHWORTH GARDEN CITY.

46. Coopers Farm in Norton Road is shown here on a postcard by an unknown publisher and posted in the first decade of the century. It had been sold to First Garden City Ltd. in 1903 and was renamed Manor Farm. It was eventually acquired and renovated by Roger Parker brother of Barry Parker.
A sleeping Porch was added at the rear which was thought to be very healthy.

OLD FARM HOUSE,
NORTON, GARDEN CITY

47. Here members of the family are shown at study in the garden of Manor Farm on another unknown publisher postcard.

THE MANOR FARM, NORTON, LETCHWORTH.   OUT-DOOR STUDY

S 6398   VIEW ON N. E. BOUNDARY, LETCHWORTH GARDEN CITY.

48. A Kingsway postcard showing Radwell in around 1910.

S 6391   COUNTY COUNCIL SCHOOLS, LETCHWORTH GARDEN CITY.

49. Norton Road School was the first County Council school to open in the Garden City on 16th October 1909. It was designed by Parker & Unwin with the classrooms set around an open courtyard allowing fresh air to circulate. The new building is shown here on a postcard by Kingsway.

50. The Picture Palace was built in 1909 in Eastcheap. It was one of the first purpose-built cinemas in the country. It was also the first building in the town centre to have electricity. It was built away from other buildings because of the fear that the nitrate film would catch fire and the Fire Station was built next door just in case ! The postcard was published by Brown & Tester.

Picture Palace, Letchworth

The Balmoral Hotel, Letchworth Herts.

BALMORAL HOTEL

51. The Balmoral Hotel in Norton Way South opposite the Paddling Pool is shown on a postcard published by Thos. B. Latchmore, of Hitchin and postmarked 1913. It was opened in 1907 and has now been converted into flats.

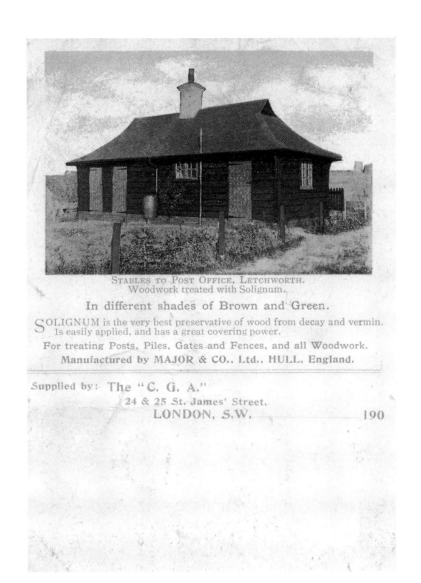

STABLES TO POST OFFICE, LETCHWORTH.
Woodwork treated with Solignum.

In different shades of Brown and Green.

SOLIGNUM is the very best preservative of wood from decay and vermin. Is easily applied, and has a great covering power.

For treating Posts, Piles, Gates and Fences, and all Woodwork.

Manufactured by MAJOR & CO., Ltd., HULL, England.

Supplied by: The "C. G. A."
24 & 25 St. James' Street,
LONDON, S.W. 190

52. Another advertising postcard for Solignum, this one issued by the Country Gentlemens Association before they were established in Letchworth. It shows the stables to the Post Office and probably dates from 1906.
Can anyone tell me exactly where this was?

FRIENDS' MEETING HOUSE.

HOWGILLS. GARDEN CITY.

53. Howgills, the Friends Meeting House in South View designed by Bennett & Bidwell was built in 1907 and financed by Miss Juliet Reckitt, the daughter of the owner of Reckitt & Colman of Hull. She also lived there in the early years. This postcard was postally used on January 1st 1910.

Baldock Road, Letchworth

54. Sheep being driven along Baldock Road (the only road to predate the Garden City) on a postcard issued by the Garden City Association and postmarked 1906. This shows how the early town combined rural and urban life.

55. The first building to house the Post Office in Letchworth was on the corner of Baldock Road and Letchworth Lane.

LETCHWORTH CORNER, GARDEN CITY

56. It was then moved to the old Estate Cottage on the corner of Spring Road and Baldock Road where it still exists. This postcard was posted in 1909.

S 1050   COMMON VIEW, LETCHWORTH.

57. On the back of this postcard of Common View before the road was surfaced is the message - "Dec. 11th 1908 My Dear how do you like him - nice figure. I am nearly settled. I find it very cold here, had a nice lady from T Centre to see me. Will write soon." The postcard was sent to Doncaster and was published by Kingsway.

58. This postcard shows 54 North Avenue and was sent by the resident to his mother. It reads - "Sunday 26.7.14. Dear Ma Hope you are keeping well am alright. Must write in a few days. Clara's sister is here for a fortnight. How do you like this photo. You never sent to tell me about your pension I hope you are getting it. Love to all Jack." It was sent to Mrs. Backhouse in Bath.

Letchworth Church

Letchworth Rectory

LETCHWORTH OLD CHURCH INTERIOR

Above

59. St. Mary's Church and Rectory shown on a Valentines Postcard. Sir Laurence Olivier lived here as a boy when his father Rev. Gerard Kerr Olivier was Rector from 1919-1926.

Above

60. The interior of St. Mary's Church on a postcard by Clutterbuck.

Left

61. The interior of St. Nicholas's Church in Norton on another postcard by Clutterbuck posted in 1910.

62. St. Michael's Church in Norton Way South was opened in 1908 and is shown on a Clutterbuck postcard. It was replaced by a new Church which opened on Broadway in 1968.

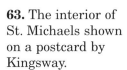

63. The interior of St. Michaels shown on a postcard by Kingsway.

64. Another postcard by Kingsway shows the interior of St. Hugh Roman Catholic Church. A larger church was later built next to it.

65. The May Day celebrations started in 1906 and are shown here on a postcard published by E. & E.H. Housden of Station Road with a Clutterbuck photograph of the 1908 fun.

66. A Kingsway postcard showing the May Festival Procession in Leys Avenue on 15th May 1909 when the May Queen was Dorothy Oxley.

67. This Clutterbuck postcard shows the May Queen and her attendants in 1912.

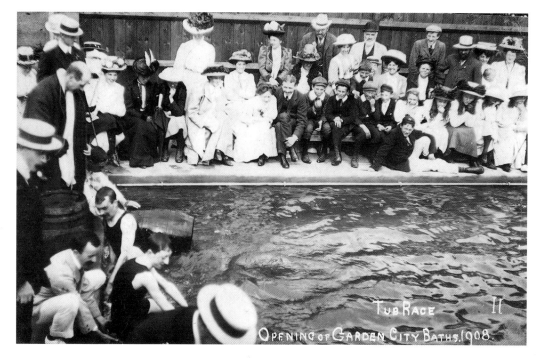

68. The first public swimming baths in the Garden City were opened in Pixmore Way by Sir Ralph Neville on Saturday 27th June 1908 followed by a Gala shown on a postcard by Clutterbuck.

69. Another Clutterbuck postcard, this one shows the private school run by J.M. Stephenson. The building became St. Christopher's School in 1933 when it moved from the site in Broadway which then became St. Francis College. Photo circa 1910.

70. The Circus at the junction of the Sollershotts and Broadway was one of the first purpose-built roundabouts for traffic in the country. It was opened on a hot summers day in 1910 when many of the waiting cars overheated. In the early days traffic was allowed to travel around the Circus in both directons. This is also a card by Clutterbuck.

Villas at Letchworth.

Above **71.**

72. Elmwood Cottages 7 & 7a Norton Way North were designed by Baillie Scott for The Cheap Cottages Exhibition but they did not qualify as their actual cost of £420 was too high. These cottages are probably the ones shown in the postcard on the front cover.

Pair of Cottages, Norton way.
(GARDEN CITY SERIES.)

Cottages, Hitchin Road.
(GARDEN CITY SERIES.)

73. These three postcards show different types of early houses around the Garden City on postcards issued by The Garden City Association, Bank Chambers, Holborn W.C.

Letchworth Hall Hotel.
(Garden City Series.)

74. An early postcard of Letchworth Hall Hotel issued by the Garden City Association. The Hall became a hotel in 1904.

It was run by the Misses Rutter who also ran the Bloomsbury Hotel in London. In 1906 the charges were - Weekly Terms from 42 shillings and weekends from 16 shillings

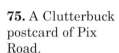

75. A Clutterbuck postcard of Pix Road.

PIX ROAD, LETCHWORTH.

76. And another one of his of Broughton Hill. Both photos were probably taken around 1910.

BROUGHTON HILL, LETCHWORTH.

77. The Tenants Hall opened 13th March 1908 and was the social centre for the Garden City tenants on the Pixmore Estate. The original hall was extended in 1912 and renamed the Pixmore Institute. It was used for performances of the Garden City Pantomimes of 1909, 10 and 11. It was also where the Inquest was held into the death of Margaret Young, aged 2 months. Her body had been discovered buried in an allotment near the railway in March 1910. The building eventually became Hillshott School. It is shown here on a Clutterbuck postcard.

78. The Annual Ball and Supper at Pixmore Institute on January 8th 1912 is shown here on a postcard sent to New England, Peterborough on January 20th 1912. Photo by W. Frost Wilson at the City Studio Letchworth.

79. Children at St. Nicholas School in Norton pose for the photographer Arthur Clutterbuck at his vantage point on the top of the tower of St. Nicholas Church. There is a Union Jack flying outside the Three Horse Shoes Public House. They could be celebrating the Coronation in 1911.

80. This postcard by Clutterbuck was sent on July 18th 1912 and shows a parade by the Boys Brigade on Hospital Sunday, raising funds for the new Hospital to be built in Letchworth.

81. This postcard, also by Clutterbuck shows the first Spirella Field Day in 1913. The girls are competing in the Departmental Tug of War.

**The development
of Station Road
and the first
shops.**

Above
82. An unmade
Station Road on a
postcard issued by
the Garden City
Association.

83/84. Two postcards issued by Valentines of early Station Road.

LEYS AVENUE, LETCHWORTH

85. A Kingsway postcard showing a half built Leys Avenue around 1908. The area where the boys are standing was developed as the Arcade, shops and the Midland Bank in the 1920's.

86. Leys Avenue in the early days. The message on this postcard reads - "How do you like this? It is the place you wrote about 2 years ago. Funny I should take it after all. E.H. Wightman". The card was postmarked 22.12.1909.

Leys Avenue, Letchworth Garden City.

87. A not quite complete Leys Avenue on a postcard by W.H. Smith.

88. A view from the new vantage point of the railway bridge opened in 1913. Looking north along Norton Way North Nevells Road is on the left and houses in Wilbury Road and Norton Road can be seen in the distance. The postcard was published by Clutterbuck and sent to Belgium in 1916.

89. This birdseye view by Clutterbuck was postally used in 1914 and shows the sheds in Nevells Road which were probably still being used by Spirella while the new factory was being built. Some houses in Icknield Way can be seen with the Common and Wilbury Road in the background.

90. This postcard by Valentines shows Bird's Hill and was used in 1907. There is a sign on the right with information about the Rushby Mead Estate.

36

Three postcards by Clutterbuck of the Hayes Reynolds Factory and Fire.

HAYES REYNOLDS WORKS, LETCHWORTH.

91. Showing the Factory and level crossing in 1912.

92. The premises on fire on May 2nd 1913.

THE FIRE AT HAYES REYNOLDS.

93. After the fire - postally used May 20th 1913. The company were calico printers in Works Road and used rotary lithographic machinery.

AMONG THE RUINS.

94/95. Two views of Norton Post Office Stores probably taken at the same time by Clutterbuck. The view below was postally used in 1914.

Two views of Norton Common by local photographer Arthur Clutterbuck who lived in Icknield Way.

Above
96. Postally used in 1912.

Right
97. Postally used in 1913.

Norton Common consists of 66 acres of public open space near the centre of town.

Three early homes in Letchworth shown on postcards:-

98. Homelia 40 Norton Road was the home of Selina Gray in 1910 on a postcard by W. Frost Wilson.

99. Harbin Cottage 127 Wilbury Road the home of Mr. Bartholemew, postally used in 1908.

100. Belle Vue 69 Norton Road. The 1911 Directory lists occupants as Oliver Barfoot, Misses Edith Bennett and E. Zompolides. Postcard by Clutterbuck shows a garden full of Hollyhocks and lavender and a ladder up against the apple loft.

Front and Reverse

101. Hitchin Road looking towards Letchworth Lane showing 'Crossways' at the corner of The Glade on an advertising postcard issued by First Garden City Ltd. and sent to the Public Record Office in 1913.

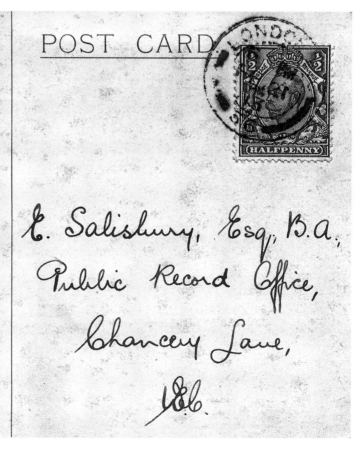

Telephone:
HOLBORN 4993.

HALTON HOUSE,
20-23, HOLBORN,
LONDON, E.C.

The Rentals of Houses at LETCHWORTH vary from cottages at 5/- or 6/- per week up to £80 per year. See view on other side. Houses also can be purchased, or land is available for building purposes, on very favourable terms. Situated on the Great Northern Railway, within an hour from London, Letchworth offers splendid advantages of residence for those desiring to get out beyond the London suburbs. Many London business people live at Letchworth, and find it cheaper than living in a London suburb. We shall be pleased to post you on further particulars and free literature if you will let us have details of your requirements.

FIRST GARDEN CITY, Ltd.

POST CARD

E. Salisbury, Esq, B.A,
Public Record Office,
Chancery Lane,
W.C.

102. This postcard by Clutterbuck was used in 1913 and shows the shops in Station Place. It carries the following message -

28/12/13 Having seen your name in the Girls Friend P.C. exchange I thought perhaps you would like to exchange some cards with me. Kindly let me know if there are any special cards you prefer. Hoping to hear from you. I remain yours etc. N. Hume., Miss Hume, 99 Ridge Avenue, Letchworth, Herts, England.

103. This postcard of Letchworth Corner Sub Post Office is also by Clutterbuck and postmarked 1914. It occupied the old 16th century cottage which stands at the junction of Hitchin and Baldock Roads and is now known as Scudamore. Raymond Unwin stayed there in 1903 while designing the layout of the Garden City. Later the estate cottage on the corner of Spring Road took over the Post Office. (See page 24).

104.

The railway had first come through Letchworth in 1850 when the line from Cambridge to Hitchin was laid. A temporary wooden station was opened in 1905 which was replaced by the new station in 1913 seen in the postcard by Clutterbuck, *above*, in the process of being built in 1912.

The Station, Garden City, Letchworth

105.

Centre

The newly opened Station on a postcard by Valentine as is this one, *right*, of Station Square, postmarked 1914 and looking towards the new Spirella building. A motor bus stands beside the Colonade, one of the earliest shopping parades in the town.

Station Square, Garden City, Letchworth

106.

107. The newly built Spirella factory on a postcard by Clutterbuck in 1914.

108. A postcard by Clutterbuck of a Training School at Spirella in August 1914.

109. The Belgian refugees arrived in Letchworth in August 1914 and are shown here in the new Spirella building on another Clutterbuck postcard. By the end of 1915 over 2000 refugees from Belgium were living in the Garden City.

Three more views by busy local photographer A. Clutterbuck.

110. This postcard was sent from Letchworth on 19th November 1916 to Belgium by Marie, probably a refugee, and shows a lonely vehicle turning into Baldock Road from Norton Way South.

111. A view of around the same time taken from Works Road shows Goods Wagons on the Railway at the empty industrial end of Icknield Way and industrial workers houses in Glebe Road and Common View.

112. This postcard was sent on 21st January 1919 and reads "How are you blowing? Nice place eh? Dad".

It shows a busy Common View including a delivery Horse and Cart.

45

113. A Clutterbuck postcard of around 1913-1914 shows the Estate Office and Post Office and the beginning of Broadway opposite the Station.

Below Two novelty postcards dating from the First World War.

114. A Valentines published Pull-Out postcard containing 16 pre-war views of Letchworth and postally used in 1917.

115. A "Humorous" postcard by J. Salmon sent from Letchworth in 1918.

Two
"Small Scotches" from LETCHWORTH

Two trusty friends I send you here,
With wishes hearty and sincere ;
And if you raise their basket bed
You'll find some charming peeps outspread. 1159

LETCHWORTH, by Night.

116. The Letchworth Peace Procession was held on October 12th 1919 and was organised by the Letchworth Branch of the National Federation of Discharged and Demobilized Sailors and Soldiers. Wreaths were laid at the Cenotaph (replaced now by the War Memorial) in Station Place and a service was held in the Town Square. Unmarked card but thought to be by Clutterbuck.

117. Pixmore Avenue Post Office and Cash Stores is shown here on a postcard by the Hitchin photographer Herbert H. Minnis and probably dates from the 1920's.

118. This Airco Aerials postcard shows an aerial view of the centre of Letchworth in the 1920's.

119. This Kingwsway view looking up Broadwater Avenue is postmarked 1927 and shows the statue of Sapho in her position from 1914 until 1936. The statue of the Greek poetess was sculpted by Thomas Maclean and given to the town by his widow in 1907. It was first placed in Lytton Avenue, soon moved to the junction of Meadow Way, then moved again to the end of Broadwater Avenue.

120. Letchworth Hall Hotel in around 1923 on another view by Clutterbuck. The Hall dates from the 15th ad 16th centuries. It became a Hotel in 1904 and the grounds became the Golf Course.

121. This Spirella published postcard was postally used in 1922 and the reverse reads - "One view of a Work Room. The conditions under which Spirella Corsets are manufactured are such as to ensure the health and efficiency of those employed in the work".

Eastcheap, Letchworth.

from top to bottom
122/123/124.
Shopping in the
Garden City in the
1920's. The Arcade
opened in 1922.

Arcade, Letchworth.

Leys Avenue and Station Place, Letchworth.

Left **125.**

Below **126.**

125/126.
Two views of
Letchworth in the
1920's published by
local retailer Bradley
Pass & Co. including
some self-publicity.

127. A postcard by
Julian A. Taylor which
shows the Norton
School May Day
Celebrations in 1923,
Blodwen Evans has
written her name on
the back.

128. The Hills family moved from North London to Letchworth in 1921 to work at Morse Chain's factory at the corner of Works Road and Pixmore Avenue. They settled in at 51 Green Lane where this photo of young Stan Hills and his mother was taken at around this time and issued as a postcard.

129. The postcard below shows the Morse Chain workers in 1928, with George and Stan Hills at the left of the middle row. I worked there in the late 1960's and some of these faces are familiar to me. They are on a photo by Latchmore of Hitchin.

130. A view showing a very rural looking Letchworth Lane on a postcard by Kingsway postmarked 1929.

131. A view of Norton Common on a postcard by an unknown publisher also postmarked 1929.

Almond Blossom, Icknield Way, Letchworth.   137

132. A postcard by an unknown publisher showing the trees in Icknield Way in blossom. The postcard was used in 1928.

BROADWAY, LETCHWORTH   577

133. A Julian A. Taylor published postcard of Broadway postmarked in 1930.

134. Air view by Aerofilms of St. Christopher's School in Broadway before it became St. Francis College in 1933.

ST. CHRISTOPHER'S SCHOOL, LETCHWORTH

BARRINGTON LODGE LETCHWORTH

135. Barrington Lodge, a small private school in Letchworth in the 1930's, on a postcard by an unknown publisher.

136. Noel Convalescent Home was founded in 1906 in Norton Way North. It later became known as the Noel Family Centre. It is shown here on a postcard published by M & E Welch, 45 Leys Avenue, Letchworth.

NOEL HOME. LETCHWORTH

Norton Way, South, Letchworth.   131

137. A view taken from the railway bridge looking up Norton Way South in the early 30's on a postcard by an unknown publisher.

138. Looking up Broadway in the 1930's showing the Police Station and the Methodist Church on a postcard issued by Bridge House and postally used in 1937.

S.16724.   BROADWAY, LETCHWORTH.

S.16723.   NORTON WAY, LETCHWORTH.

139. Another Bridge House postcard showing Norton Way South in the 1930's.

55

ST. HELENS, LETCHWORTH.

143. St. Helen's Toddlers Convalescent Home in Norton Way North shown on a postcard by Bradley Pass and postmarked in 1935.

144. The new Swimming Pool was built on the edge of Norton Common and opened in August 1935. It is shown here on a postcard by Valentines.

G. 4968.   THE SWIMMING POOL, LETCHWORTH.

EASTCHEAP. LETCHWORTH.   CLS.

145. The second cinema in Letchworth designed by Bennett & Bidwell was opened in 1935. This view looking down Eastcheap also shows the Palace Cinema and the Fire Station on a postcard by an unknown publisher from the 1930's.

146. A Julian A. Taylor published postcard of the Spirella factory and gardens in the 1930's.

147. On the back of this postcard is written -
'Published by the Spirella Corset Factory, Letchworth (Garden City) Herts.
A view of the cutting department. Skilled cutters are employed in this branch of the manufacture of Spirella Corsets, which are made to order and supplied only through trained corsetieres, to the individual requirements of clients'.

148. A view of Willian Way on a postcard by M & L National Series postmarked 1948.

149. Scenes around town in the 1950's on a multi-view by Valentines postmarked 1956.

150. Station Place and the War Memorial in the 1950's on a postcard also by Valentines.

151. A multi-view of Letchworth in the 1960's on a postcard by M & L National Series.

152. A quiet Hitchin Road looking towards the Old Post Office and Baldock Road shown on a postcard by W. Bourne, Leicester.

153. The Spirella factory with gardens in full bloom in 1962 celebrating 52 years of Spirella in Letchworth.

154. A Friths published multi-view from around 1960.

Above & right
155/156. Two views of Letchworth town centre published by M & L.

157. A view of Letchworth Grammar School situated in Broadway opposite Town Square in the 1960's on a postcard published by Valentines.

158. A postcard published by Aerofilms and Aeropictorial in the 1960's shows Willian School and house building on the new Jackmans Estate.

159/160. Two postcards by an unknown publisher of St. Francis' College probably dating from the 1960's.

161.
Norton Post Office.

162. The Manor House, Norton.

Two postcards of drawings by Bernard Bellringer, a local Artist.

163. Nortonbury Scout and Guide Activity Centre opened in 1979 in the former farmhouse on a site inhabited since Saxon times. The drawing is by Ken Johnson and was published by Letchworth and Baldock District Scouts.

164. A multi-view of the town centre in the 1970's by Photo Precision.

above Saffron Hill
below Norton Village
Published by Judges in the 1970's

John F. Kennedy Gardens
Roundabout, Norton Way South.

Eastcheap, Letchworth L.2105

top to bottom
166/167/168.
Around the town in
the 1970's.

Leys Avenue, Letchworth L.2101

Howard Park, Letchworth L.2103

WILBURY ROAD (designed by Brodie 1905)

169. 158 Wilbury Road was an entry in the 1905 Exhibition. It was constructed of pre-fabricated concrete slabs cast in Liverpool and transported by train to Letchworth. It was erected in 36 hours. The house was designed by John Brodie, Liverpool City Engineer.

WILBURY ROAD (former Round House designed by Hesketh & Stokes 1905)

170. The Round House' was one of the most unusual exhibits in the 1905 exhibition. It was designed by Hesketh & Stokes for Cubitts and was constructed of pre-fabricated reinforced concrete panels and formed a 16 sided structure. Panels were cast on site. It as occupied until 1986 by which time the structure had deteriorated so much that the family had to move out and it had disintegrated by 1987.

ICKNIELD WAY (designed by Bennett & Bidwell 1905)

171. 221 Icknield Way designed by Bennett & Bidwell won second prize in the Cheap Cottages Exhibition. Arthur Clutterbuck the prolific local photographer and his family lived here. His daughters took over the family photographic business when he died in 1939.

STANDALONE FARM

172. Local children enjoying a visit to Standalone Farm.

EASTCHEAP

173. An updated Eastcheap in the town centre.

THE WYND

174. and a much modernised Wynd.

PLINSTON HALL

175. The new community hall in Broadway opened in June 1982.

RUSHBY MEAD (designed by Bennett & Bidwell 1911)

176. The gardens of Rushby Mead in the 1980's.

SAPPHO, HOWARD GARDEN

177. The end of a long and varied journey for Sapho in the Ball Memorial Garden in Howard Park where it stood from 1936 until it was stolen in the 1990's.

LETCHWORTH GATE

178. No apologies for this card which could win an award for the most boring in the book.

BROADWAY IN THE SNOW

179/180. Two contrasting views of the Garden City from the 1980's.
All the Postcards on pages 67-72 were originally published in 1980's by Letchworth Garden City Corporation in the form of a calendar.

BIRDS HILL COTTAGES

181. Around the town centre in the 1990's on a postcard by Halcyon.

182. Norton Village in the 1990's on a postcard by Judges.

Letchworth
the world's first garden city

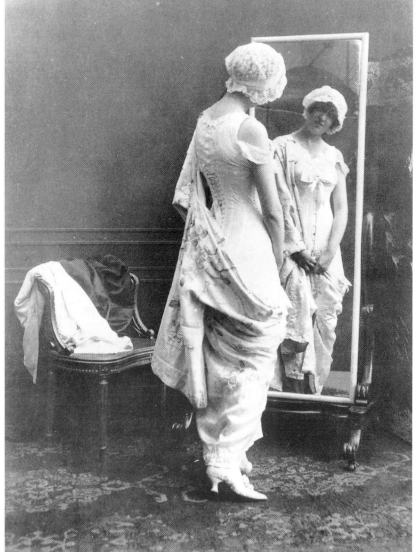

Above
183. The First Garden City Heritage Museum in Norton Way South was originally the home and office of Garden City architect Barry Parker on a postcard issued by Judges.

Left
184. A publicity photograph issued by the Spirella Company in 1912 and put on a postcard by First Garden City Heritage Museum.

74

185. Standalone Farm is a traditional working farm standing in 170 acres and only 15 minutes walk from the town centre. It is open to the public from April to September. This postcard was published by Halcyon of Bushey.

186. Jacob Ewe and Lamb at Standalone Farm on a postcard published by Noel Tatt Ltd

187. A publicity postcard issued by the Home Extension Team, a company from Hitchin showing some of their projects in Letchworth.

188. A view of Letchworth Garden City on a multi-view postcard of Hertfordshire published by E.T. W Dennis in the 1990's.

189. A poster issued by First Garden City Ltd. in 1906 shown a postcard issued by First Garden City Heritage Museum.

190. One of Letchworth's black squirrels on a postcard issued by Letchworth Museum & Art Gallery. Photograph by Brian Sawford.

191. The Cloisters, Barrington Road shown on a postcard issued by Judges is now the Masonic headquarters in Hertfordshire.

192. Willian Pond also on a postcard by Judges.

LETCHWORTH

193. Commerce Way, Letchworth town Centre in the 1990's published by E.T.W. Dennis.

194. Laying the copper roof, St. Michael's, Letchworth 1967 by Robin Mackertich. Issued by Letchworth Museum and Art Gallery in the 1990's.

then **195.** Looking down Leys Avenue in around 1908 on a postcard by Valentines

and now **196.** Looking down Leys Avenue in around 1968 on a postcard by Photo Precision

INDEX

61	Norton Church, Interior	Clutterbuck
62	St. Michaels & All Angels Church, Letchworth Garden City	Clutterbuck
63	Interior of St. Michael's Church, Letchworth Garden City	Kingsway
64	Interior of St. Hugh (R.C.) Church, Letchworth	Kingsway
65	May Day 1908	Clutterbuck
66	May Day Procession, Garden City, 1908	Kingsway
67	The May Queen with attendants, Letchworth 1912	Clutterbuck
68	Tub Race, opening of Garden City Baths 1908	Clutterbuck
69	Letchworth Private Schools	Clutterbuck
70	The Circus, Sollershott, Letchworth	Clutterbuck
71	Villas at Letchworth	Garden City Association
72	Pair of Cottages, Norton Way	Garden City Association
73	Cottages, Hitchin Road	Garden City Association
74	Letchworth Hall Hotel	Garden City Association
75	Pix Road, Letchworth	Clutterbuck
76	Broughton Hill, Letchworth	Clutterbuck
77	Pixmore Institute, Letchworth	Clutterbuck
78	Pixmore Annual 8.1.12	W. Frost Wilson
79	From the Church Tower, Norton	Clutterbuck
80	Hospital Sunday, Letchworth	Clutterbuck
81	Spirella Field Day 1913	Clutterbuck
82	Station Temperance Hotel, from Station Road	Garden City Association
83	Station Road, Garden City, Letchworth	Valentines
84	Station Road, Letchworth Garden City	Valentines
85	Leys Avenue, Letchworth	Kingsway
86	Leys Avenue	Publisher Unknown
87	Leys Avenue, Letchworth Garden City	W.H. Smith
88	Norton Way North, Letchworth	Clutterbuck
89	Birdseye view of Letchworth	Clutterbuck
90	Bird's Hill, Garden City, Letchworth	Valentines
91	Hayes Reynolds Works, Letchworth	Clutterbuck
92	The Fire at Hayes Reynolds	Clutterbuck
93	Among the ruins	Clutterbuck
94	The Post Office, Norton	Clutterbuck
95	The Post Office, Norton	Clutterbuck
96	Icknield Way from Common, Letchworth	Clutterbuck
97	Norton Common	Clutterbuck
98	40 Norton Road	W. Frost Wilson
99	127 Wilbury Road	Publisher Unknown
100	69 Norton Road	Clutterbuck
101	First Garden City Advertisement	First Garden City Ltd.
102	Station Place, Letchworth	Clutterbuck
103	Letchworth Corner Sub Post Office	Clutterbuck
104	Birds Eye View of Letchworth	Clutterbuck
105	The Station, Garden City, Letchworth	Valentine
106	Station Square, Garden City, Letchworth	Valentine
107	Spirella	Clutterbuck
108	Fourth National Spirella Training School, Letchworth, England Aug. 17-22 1914	Clutterbuck
109	Our Belgian visitors at 'The Spirella'	Clutterbuck
110	Norton Way South, Letchworth	Clutterbuck
111	View from Works Road, Letchworth	Clutterbuck
112	Common View, Letchworth	Clutterbuck
113	The Broadway, Letchworth	Clutterbuck
114	Two "Small Scotches" from Letchworth	Valentine
115	Letchworth, by night	J. Salmon
116	Letchworth Peace Procession	probably Clutterbuck
117	Pixmore Avenue Post Office & Cash Stores	Herbert G. Minnis, Hitchin
118	Leys Avenue, Letchworth from the air	Airco Aerials
119	Broadwater Avenue, Letchworth Garden City	Kingsway
120	Letchworth Hall Hotel	Clutterbuck
121	Workroom Spirella	Spirella Corset Factory
122	Eastcheap, Letchworth	Publisher Unknown
123	Arcade, Letchworth	Publisher Unknown

124	Leys Avenue and Station Place, Letchworth	Publisher Unknown
125	Common View, Letchworth	Bradley Pass & Co.
126	Leys Avenue, Letchworth	Bradley Pass & Co.
127	May Day 1923, Norton School	Julian A. Taylor
128	51 Green Lane, Letchworth	Hills Family
129	Workers at Morse Chain	Latchmore of Hitchin
130	Letchworth Lane	Kingsway
131	The Common, Letchworth	Publisher Unknown
132	Almond Blossom, Icknield Way, Letchworth	Publisher Unknown
133	Broadway, Letchworth	Julian A. Taylor
134	St. Christopher's School, Letchworth	Aerofilms
135	Barrington Lodge, Letchworth	Publisher Unknown
136	Noel Home, Letchworth	M & E Welch
137	Norton Way, South, Letchworth	Publisher Unknown
138	Broadway, Letchworth	Bridge House
139	Norton Way, Letchworth	Bridge House
140	4 picture multi-view	Valentines
141	5 picture multi-view	Valentines
142	4 picture multi-view	Valentines
143	St. Helens, Letchworth	Bradley Pass
144	The Swimming Pool, Letchworth	Valentines
145	Eastcheap, Letchworth	Publisher Unknown
146	The Fountain, Spirella Gardens, Letchworth	Julian A. Taylor
147	Spirella Cutting Dept.	Spirella Corset Factory
148	Willian Way, Letchworth	M & L National Series
149	7 picture multi-view	Valentines
150	Station Place and War Memorial	Valentines
151	4 picture multi-view	M & L National Series
152	Letchworth Corner, Letchworth	W. Bourne, Leicester
153	Spirella Factory Gardens in bloom	Spirella Corset Factory
154	5 picture multi view	Friths
155	Leys Avenue, Letchworth	M & L National Series
156	Eastcheap, Letchworth	M & L National Series
157	The Grammar School, Letchworth	Reproduced by kind permission Hallmark Cards.
158	The Willian School, Letchworth	Aerofilms & Aeropictorial
159	Inner Courtyard, St. Francis College, Letchworth	Publisher Unknown
160	Cricket Ground, St. Francis College, Letchworth	Publisher Unknown
161	Norton Post Office	Bernard Bellringer
162	The Manor House, Norton	Bernard Bellringer
163	Norton Bury Activity Centre	Letchworth & Baldock District Scouts
164	4 picture multi-view	Photo Precision
165	4 picture multi-view	Courtesy Judges Postcards Ltd.
166	Eastcheap, Letchworth	Publisher Unknown
167	Leys Avenue, Letchworth	Publisher Unknown
168	Howard Park, Letchworth	Publisher Unknown
169	158 Wilbury Road	Letchworth Garden City Corporation
170	Wilbury Road (Former Round House)	Letchworth Garden City Corporation
171	221 Icknield Way	Letchworth Garden City Corporation
172	Standalone Farm	Letchworth Garden City Corporation
173	Eastcheap	Letchworth Garden City Corporation
174	The Wynd	Letchwoth Garden City Corporation
175	Plinston Hall	Letchworth Garden City Corporation
176	Rushby Mead	Letchworth Garden City Corporation

197. After the fire in Croft Lane. Message reads "The three children I have put a spot on are the ones I used to look after" and is unsigned. This postcard was published by Clutterbuck around 1910.